The OOEY GOOEY Handbook

2006

Published by
The Learning Through Adventure Company
Rochester, New York

The Learning Through Adventure Company
Rochester, New York
toll free (800) 477-7977
www.ooeygooey.com

ISBN # 0-9706634-0-4

Photographs contributed by:
Lisa Murphy
Michael Griffen
CéCé Canton
Kimberly Griffen

"What's going on here?!"—Wolf Illustration
© 2002 Michelle Murphy

Cover and Book Design
Andrew Curl

2001 and 2002 Printings
Printed in the United States

2005 Printing
Printed in China

The OOEY GOOEY Handbook

This book is dedicated to all the families, children and teachers I have worked with through the years.

A Note To You From Lisa.....

In her book, *Teaching in the Key of Life*, author Mimi Bronsky-Chenfeld talks about the "wolves" that are occasionally seen stalking school hallways and lurking around preschool classroom doors. Wolves, by definition, are those concerned types who want to know what children are "doing" all day (read: doing to get ready for kindergarten). They desire to know the rationale for flubber, the developmentally appropriateness of ooblick, the reason for the hokey pokey, the goal of splatter painting, and the objective of swinging on your tummy. They seem to search incessantly for an overall justification of the importance of what we might call "play".

Great will be the day when we no longer have to defend what we do – but for now, we do. Therefore, we must be armed with an arsenal of information. And while we fight as we might to have play valued for it's own sake, we have the professional responsibility to be able to articulate what is happening when children do play. When children are engaged in meaningful experiences and spend time in environments that emphasize wonder, discovery and creativity, (not the accumulation of a bunch o'facts) "learning" is happening all day long! Unfortunately though, many of us work in environments where there is a lot of pressure for children to be performing, gathering random bits of knowledge and hurrying up to be "ready" for the next expectation with no time left to appreciate the here-and-now. As professionals we must work towards being able to convey our message about the value of play to the "wolves" that come to our door.

I have found, amazingly enough, that sometimes all it takes are a few strategically placed phrases such as, "when we are squeezing playdough we are strengthening our hands and eventually, when our hands and fingers are strong enough, we are able to hold pencils", or "when we make ooblick we are exploring the difference between solids and liquids" to ease fears and worries that the children aren't doing anything.

So when it came time to move ahead with the second printing of the *Ooey Gooey Handbook* we asked ourselves, do we simply print off more copies or do we take the time to make some changes and add the "wolf words"?? We opted to make the additions and include them in this second printing in order to assist you in articulating what is happening in your classrooms, living rooms, kitchens and family child care homes.

Hands-on learning is the most appropriate way for young children to explore and learn about their world. Some people understand this immediately - some do not. Some start out as wolves, questioning, challenging and demanding. Please know that the parents who "get it" might be easier to deal with, but the wolves are on your side too! They just require something more - something different - in order to truly embrace the importance of child-centered environments. They want to know that you know what you are doing! When the children are finger painting and they ask what the children are doing and why, they appreciate it when you are able to go deeper than "it's so much fun!" Yes, it is fun! However, finger painting also increases small motor coordination, facilitates pre-writing skills and serves as a medium for children to progress through the many stages of scribbling. Verbiage fluff? Not to the parent who needs this from you. We need to know our stuff! Really - you DO know these things!! It's just that when we feel on the spot, flustered, or are distracted by twenty children, we might forget.

So we included them here to help you remember. At the bottom of each Ooey Gooey activity page we have included some of the concepts which can be applied to the experience. This way *everyone* can continue developing and deepening their understanding of the importance of creating hands-on, child-centered early childhood environments. It is my wish that these additions might assist you as you work together creating magical, engaging places for children and their families.

All my best to you.
Love,

The Ooey Gooey Lady
October 2002

8

Acknowledgements:

Thank you to Carolyn, Sarah, Judy, Susan, Tami, Kathleen and Tom for your collective wisdom and support, patience and suggestions, editing hours and input as I transferred what was in my head and heart onto paper.

Thank you to Cynde for being my mentor and inspiration as I began my journey. Even though you are far away I think of you often. Your stay in California was short and sweet, but I know you were brought out here for a reason. Thank you for being my guide, my friend and my Obi-Wan.

To Miss Mary - Thank you for back porches, piñatas, real hammers, freshly made butter on saltines, *Mike Mulligan and His Steam Shovel*, hours in the mud, books in the bathroom, a clay room, upright pianos, pepper jack cheese, ducks in the yard and a big boat to paint. I do what I do because of you - thank you.

INTRODUCTION

I have dedicated my professional life to creating places where children can simply "be." Where they can engage in experiences that are meaningful to them and have long periods of uninterrupted free time. Where teachers are encouraged to facilitate, instead of "teach." Where preschool is not boot camp for kindergarten. Where it is believed that preschoolers do not need bite-sized morsels of an elementary school curriculum and where the curiosity and wonder of childhood is free flowing.

I do what I do because of the nursery school experience I had, and I know in my heart of hearts I was put here to give that back. It is my passion, dream and goal to develop places where children can be immersed in all the things that symbolize childhood: mud, sand, water, paint, blocks, songs, books, frogs, trucks, forts, tree houses, tires and ropes. I am forever creating places that provide children with the time, space, materials, and support they need to simply be children and I hope this book encourages you to do the same.

This book was written for everyone who works with children; kindergarten teachers, parents, family childcare providers, principals, playgroup captains, administrators, grandparents, teachers' aides and preschool teachers. May it assist you as you increase your understanding of what "child-centered" means, as you plan exciting activities for the children in your care and as you create and promote environments that encourage a love of life-long learning.

CONTENTS

THE JOURNEY BEGINS

Unofficially, I am a binkie finder, marble painter, cartwheel turner, back patter, song singer, diaper changer, story writer, skinned knee fixer, cold coffee drinker, PBJ eater, problem solver, hand holder, paint cup filler, grass stain fighter, tree climber, block builder, puddle splasher, hokey pokey dancer and mud pie baker.

Officially, I am a teacher.

I became a teacher because of one particular woman. Miss Mary. Miss Mary owned a Nursery School in Livermore, California. And, in the early 1970's, I was fortunate to have been one of her students. I can remember my days at Mary's better than I can remember days at junior high and even high school! While I was studying Early Childhood Education in college, there was never any doubt in my mind that I was put here on this earth to give what I got back. My vision of Early Childhood Education meant being able to create places where children could have the same adventure filled mornings I was fortunate enough to have had. Mornings filled with painting, clay, blocks, songs, stories, mud pies, dress up, big shovels and real hammers, bikes, water, lots of outdoor time and plenty of open-ended experiences within hours of free play.

Upon graduation from college I quickly learned that the idealism of Mary's had been replaced by the reality of day care. I showed up for my

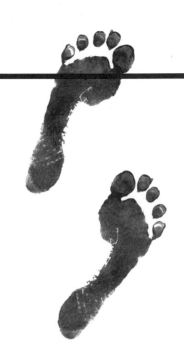

first day of teaching preschool and was told to have my lesson plans and ditto request form on the director's desk every Friday by noon. In addition, I was "teamed up" with a teacher who had a timer to tell the children when to "switch" activities, thick rows of masking tape line-up lines all over the floor, name tags on the children, a "think about it chair," a whistle around her neck, and lesson plans that were laminated from 1975.

Giving back what I got was not going to be as easy as I thought.

I wondered both aloud and silently where the easels were, wondered why we only had thirty minutes of outside time when the children were often there for six, eight, eleven hours, and wondered why we had to do dittos. I shared a few of my concerns and thoughts with the other teachers, and was told, "Lisa, we have to do curriculum now to get the kids ready for kindergarten! Make sure you send an art project home each day, but be sure not to let them get too dirty - always use the smocks. Make some name tags for the lunch table – and always label your bulletin boards, the parents want to know what they did each day. And, oh, at nap time, never rub backs for more than 10 minutes – it throws the lunches off. Be sure to come in from the play yard when your time is up and make sure they don't have too much 'center time' - you can't just let them play all day, face it Lisa, it's not the 70's anymore - you better just get with the program."

And because I lacked the strength and confidence to question what they told me, I did what they told me to do.

I made masking tape line-up lines and name tags for the children to show them where to sit for circle time and lunch. I said things like, "Shh, be quiet," "Inside voices please" and "Stop running." I had beautiful bulletin boards (that I created) covered with product oriented art, I followed my schedule *to the minute*, and had laminated STOP signs to tell the children when a certain area of the classroom was "closed" and "off limits." I planned curriculum based around weekly themes and monthly holidays and sang a whole bunch of songs that were all to the tune of "Jingle Bells" and "Row Row Row Your Boat."

It took three years of "getting with the program" before I realized that the program wasn't working for me or for the children. The journey of "changing my mind" took a long time, journeys usually do. I started to question everything I did. I wondered how my actions, words and behaviors impacted the children. I wondered how I influenced and/or stifled their curiosity, creativity and sense of wonder. Was I really giving back what I had experienced at Mary's? Or, had I sold out to the pressure of getting with the program?

CHANGING MY MIND

I answered my own question during a frenzied fall morning when my new team teacher, Cynde, watched me go crazy while I attempted to complete a "small-medium-large" project I had planned for the children. Of course, since it was October, I had spent the previous evening cutting out various sizes of orange construction paper "pumpkins" so that I could teach twelve, three year olds about size by having them glue the pumpkins on their paper in order from big to little. I brought the pumpkins (and even the little green stems) into class and began telling the children how to do it, but all they wanted to do was squeeze the glue out! They were not doing it "right" and I was getting very frustrated!

My lesson plans said that today we were going to learn about "small-medium-large" but all these children wanted to learn about was how to empty glue bottles! I was going to use this project to decorate the bulletin board! But how was I going to fill up the holiday board with this holiday art if all they wanted to do was pile the pumpkins all on top of one another? The projects didn't even look right! You couldn't even tell that they were pumpkins!

I was still getting upset. To make it worse, while the kids were "creating," I kept saying things like, "NO NO NO NO! STOP STOP STOP! YOU ARE USING TOO MUCH GLUE – HERE, WATCH ME!" I was totally and completely destroying any shred of creativity this project ever had. The children were getting up and leaving the art table. Who can blame them? They were determined to find something in the room that actually interested them. I was frantically cutting out more pumpkins and more stems, begging the children to "please come back and make one more. It's for the board! Come make one for your mom!" when Cynde stood up. She walked over to me, and calmly said, "I could never understand why a teacher would spend more time preparing a project than the children would actually spend doing it."

I stopped. I looked up from my cutting, directly at her. I glanced over at her children. They were all engaged, painting at the easel, building with Legos and blocks, reading books, coloring with crayons and paper, and playing dress-up. I looked at my children. They were running around the room. I was begging them to come back to the table to "make one more," hollering at them to just use "a little bit of glue" and to "watch me," so they would do it right.

In the middle of it all Cynde was quite literally telling me to **_cut it out!_** A light bulb went off in my head and I had my first career changing AH-HA!

BEING READY

If you take what Cynde said out of context, it wasn't anything major or profound. What she said made an impact because I WAS FINALLY READY TO HEAR IT. I'll never know how many gems she placed in my path prior to that moment, because up until that time, I simply was not ready to receive them. It is said that when the student is ready, the teacher will appear. I was finally ready and Cynde was there for me. She guided and assisted me as I began the journey of rediscovering the teaching style that was in my heart.

TAKING YOUR TIME

In the movie *Star Wars*, Obi Wan Kanobi says to Luke Skywalker, "You have taken your first step into a larger world." This statement also rings true for us as we start our journey leading into the world of child-centered teaching. More than likely, you will not read this book and say, "That's it! I did it! I'm so child-centered!"

The journey takes time. It involves a lot of self exploration. We must examine the ideas, values, attitudes, likes, dislikes, etc, that we bring along with us. Becoming child-centered means questioning, reading, examining, challenging and rethinking what we have always been doing.

Take baby steps. If you do too much too soon you will get frustrated. If some of the activities and philosophical concepts presented in this book are new for you, do not start changing everything on Monday morning! Take your time. Don't rush it. At the same time, if you find you are doing something right now that you just can't believe you've been doing, and you say to yourself, "Oh my gosh I can't believe that I do that!" and you want to stop doing it, then do just that, STOP it. Don't feel guilty, just cut it out!

If I continued to brood about all the years I said things like, "sit-still-be-quiet-hands-home-get-in-line-inside-voices-stop-running-get-out-of-the-water" I'd be miserable. I refer to my first few years of teaching, as "before I knew better." Give yourself permission to change your mind.

I realize that some of you reading this are not in the position to start making major changes within your environment. Teaching is a cooperative effort between teachers, co-teachers, aides, helpers, assistants, parents, administration, directors, principals and owners. Rules, policies and guidelines within preschools are often NOT created by the people working with the children. If your floor is carpeted, your director or owner might be concerned about easel painting, playing with playdough or having a water table. If you share a space with another group or organization there may be concerns about cleanliness or clean up policies. If you have a team teacher with a different teaching style than you, there may be objections and questions to some of the activities presented in the curriculum portion of the book. Do the best you can while still growing, changing and continuing on your journey.

CHILD-CENTERED IS NOT CHAOS!

The next section will outline how to identify and create child-centered environments, but before that we must have a grasp on what the term "child-centered" means. Over the years, I have learned that "child-centered" has a different definition depending on the group of people who are discussing the word. To some teachers and directors the term "child-centered" conjures up images of a classroom that looks like *Lord of the Flies* with children running around half naked with paint flying through the air! To some parents, it means that children are allowed to "do what they want" with no interaction or involvement from the teacher.

This is NOT being child-centered, but rather, being disengaged. At the same time, putting out three new activity ideas you just learned at a conference on Saturday, as you turn around and do the bulletin board, is not being child-centered either.

Child-centered teaching is NOT chaos! It does NOT mean the absence of rules, structure, boundaries or curriculum. It means that as an early childhood educator you realize the power of play and the importance of creativity. It means you respect children's individual developmental timetables and that you have an understanding of the research that impacts our profession.

Child-centered teaching is the hardest way to be. WHY?? Because teachers who embrace this philosophy realize that there is NOT a one-size-fits-all formula that will fit each child each time in each situation. Educators and parents are often on the hunt for the perfect "If this, do that" program. We think that finding such a formula will make our jobs easier. We want to know what to do with the child who _____(insert your favorite behavior here). We then attempt to apply this one formula to each child who engages in this behavior. When it doesn't work, we get frazzled and upset, so we begin a *new* search for a *better* formula. Please permit me to save you a lot of time, money and headache by telling you, in all honesty, there isn't one out there. When you try to fit twelve individual children into an all encompassing, one-size-fits-all formula, you create nothing more than a recipe for frustration and disaster for both you and the children.

Child-centered teachers are the most dedicated, passionate and committed educators I know. They have realized through self exploration, reading, experience and continued personal and professional growth, that creating environments which facilitate exploration, cultivate creativity, encourage wonder and problem solving, are environments that plant the seeds for a love of life long learning.

IDENTIFYING A CHILD-CENTERED ENVIRONMENT

Although there are other indicators of a child-centered place, I have listed here the four essential ones: long periods of uninterrupted free time, few restrictions, adults acting as facilitators and lots of outdoor time. The next few pages will talk about each of them separately.

Identifying Characteristic #1
LONG PERIODS OF UNINTERRUPTED FREE TIME

I have worked in places where teachers have worn whistles around their necks and shuffled children from one "center" to another. I have interviewed in places where children move (at the teachers will, not theirs) from the art room to the block room to the science room to the clay room. I have watched teachers set timers, allowing each child 5 minutes of interaction with an "enrichment activity" (table top toys, folder games, puzzles, pegs, math cubes, bead stringing) then promptly announce "SWITCH!" at which time the children would stop what they were doing and methodically move to the seat to their right. *Preschool is not boot camp for kindergarten.* Classroom management techniques such as these do not encourage learning. They encourage the continuation of the belief that the teacher knows everything, is in complete control and children will do what they are told.

This mind set does not honor individual time tables or allow for in-depth explorations. Rushed and over programmed days hinder problem solving, a love of lifelong learning, creative thinking and self-sufficiency. When children are told from infancy until kindergarten when to eat, sleep, pee, poop, line up, go outside, come back in; when their playtime is sectioned into twenty minute time blocks with teachers telling them what and where they can "play," and, when they are shuffled (herded) from one activity to another, they go on to elementary school not knowing how to make decisions, not knowing how to think for themselves, and, as I'm sure you have seen, not knowing how to play.

Twenty minutes of free play is NOT a long time. Nor is it enough time. Imagine for a minute your most favorite thing to do. What is it? Reading? Photography? Sewing? Gardening? Long walks? Painting? Writing poetry? Cooking? Singing? Baking cakes? Now imagine that someone tells you to "go play." You drop what you're doing and run to the kitchen, or your sewing room, the garden, the darkroom. Stopping on the way to read a piece of mail, answer a phone call, grab your materials, hat, tools, bowls, fabric, camera. Get to your destination; settle into your recent project only to be told, "OK! Time's up! Clean up!"

You'd say, "WHAT?! I haven't even started yet! I haven't even played yet! I didn't even *do* anything!" How would you feel? What do you think would happen if you were constantly being subjected to this start stop pattern? What do you think would happen to your desire to "play?" More than likely, it would cease. Eventually you might be told, "go play," but you would not run to the garden anymore, or the kitchen or the library, because you just wouldn't want to bother. This is what children do when we do not give them enough time to play and explore.

It happens to children everyday in our attempt to "stay on schedule."

I have seen children run run run to the easel only to be barked at by the teacher en route; "push up your sleeves," "that's not your paper," "it's clean up time, you can do that later," "watch out for your shoes," "get a smock." I have seen children scurry into their classroom and run to the block area. All ready to dump the blocks out to make a big castle, only to be told, "don't dump that out," "don't expect anyone to help you if you dump all those blocks out," "don't start that now, we're getting ready for lunch." When these are the messages children receive, and when their interests are not facilitated and encouraged by their teachers, providers and parents, they will stop playing. After a time they will cease running to the easel and the block area, just as you would stop running to the sewing room. We unknowingly kill their curiosity.

You know from your own experience that some children need twenty minutes just to decide where they want to play! Then, after thirty or forty minutes of play when you announce, "CLEAN UP!!" the children who have been playing look at you and say, "WHAT? I just started what do you mean clean up??" The other half has been standing around doing nothing because the pattern has already been set that there is never enough time, so they just don't bother anymore. They look at you and say, "Well I didn't play with anything so I'm not going to clean up." Ouch.

Children need time to wallow in their experiences and to "get lost" in their activities. An hour is a good starting spot. They need a beginning, middle and an end. Otherwise, we are creating a generation of procrastinators. These children will have no follow-through because they were never given enough time to explore, play, complete a project or an idea, or pursue their interests.

Having long periods of uninterrupted free time is an essential criterion of a child-centered place. Teachers tell me that long periods of free time are not going to happen at their schools because they have to follow a schedule. They want to know when the kids are doing art, science, counting and reading. So do their directors. My answer is that all of these things are going on all the time, but instead of saying art at 8:00, math at 8:20, reading at 8:40, snack at 9:00 and outside at 9:15 we might arrange our schedule to say that from 8:00 – 9:15 we have inside time. Then the environment is prepared in such a way that the children are able to play math games, read stories, paint pictures, scribble with markers, build with blocks, scoop the sand or create with clay during the entire block of time. The children's inside explorations are not chopped up into twenty-minute time blocks.

When asked, "Do you have a schedule?" I say, "Yes, we have a schedule. The kids arrive at 7:00, we eat lunch around noonish, and most of them go home between 4:00 and 5:00."

We don't "do" art on Tuesday because that's when I feel like dragging the easel out – the easel is always out for children to paint whenever they want. We don't "do" science at 10:30 three days a week - we are sciencing all day long because the environment is always filled with experiences that encourage exploration of scientific principles, magnets, water, colors, eyedroppers and magnifying glasses. We don't "do" music on Friday's because that's when the "Music Man" consultant comes in and sings TO the children instead of WITH them, we are instead singing and chanting and playing with musical instruments all day long.

At our school there is an art area, a science area, a reading area, a free art area, two sensory tubs (one wet, one dry), a block area and a puzzle and manipulative area. Outside there are also art, water and bubble areas, and mud, sand and climbing opportunities. During gathering time, children can come to the carpet for stories and songs if they want to. Some listen as they are reading in the book area, some listen while squishing playdough at a table; others are on the carpet with me singing. During snack time some children eat and some don't. It is ok if they don't eat because they know if they come up later and say, "I'm hungry" they will be given crackers or fruit. And although our program permits children to play in or out as they please, if you are in more of a structured "center" environment, try to make sure your outside time is never less than sixty minutes.

At our school, when the kids are playing inside, time is NOT chopped up into segments for various projects or explorations, such as math, reading, art or science. Instead, when children are playing inside, they are permitted all the time they need (they don't go home until 4:00) to get engaged with an activity and experience the beginning, middle and end I mentioned earlier. Children choose what they want to do within the environment that was prepared prior to their arrival. Activities such as: art, blocks, legos, puzzles, manipulatives, dress-up, sensory tubs and science experiments are available on a daily basis.

Because I provide long periods of uninterrupted free playtime I do not have a lot of behavior problems. The children are able to move and explore freely. There isn't pressure to hurry and/or clean up. I honor the power of time and the idea of a beginning, middle and end to a play session. I have seen too many children stop playing because they were worried about when it was going to be clean up time. Additionally, I do not have behavior problems because I fill the environment with experiences meaningful to the children: open-ended and play based. We might have *twelve* children in the class—but we have enough going on to keep *twenty* engaged. And most importantly, I do not have behavior problems because I control the environment, not the little people in it.

The cornerstones of truly child-centered place are long periods of free time to get engaged, to wallow in experiences, to repeat behaviors in order to master developmental skills and to have time to be curious and develop a passion for discovery.

Using **real** tools is so exciting for children!

Identifying Characteristic #2
FEW RESTRICTIONS

The mindset and belief here is that it is our job to control the environment, not the little people in it. It is my goal to create a YES-YES environment where I can say YES (instead of the ever popular NO NO NO NO) as often as possible. I am able to do this in two ways: The first, arriving at school earlier than the children, to set up the space so it is ready for them as soon as they walk in the door. The second, by questioning the list of rules I might be attempting to enforce.

Prior to the children's arrival it is essential that you have already done the work! By setting up the room before the children arrive you can greet them at the door saying "good morning, good morning, come on in, good to see you." The reason you can do this is because you have already put out the crayons and paper, paper up on the easel, playdough out on a table, water colors out on a table, sand in a sensory tub and cornstarch in another, whatever! The environment is ready for the kids so that you can be 100% in tune with welcoming them into the space. Jenna Yates, a 2nd grade teacher in Southern California can relate! She recently told me that,

> "In order for me to be a successful teacher, I need to be prepared. I arrive at school an hour early each day to physically and mentally prepare. If I don't feel 100%

organized when I start my day, then usually the rest of the day feels rushed and my teaching suffers. Teacher preparedness affects the students and their performance. If you are ready, then they are ready."

As teachers and providers you know that the first twenty minutes will set the tone for the rest of the day. If you spend that introductory time running around, trying to get snack ready, taking the chairs down off the table, filling paint cups, getting markers out, filling up the water table, warming up a bottle, getting the infants down for their first nap you will be frustrated, exhausted and will feel fifteen minutes behind all day long! Make a commitment to prepare the room before they get there. This way you can be 100% in tune with the children instead of running around trying to get things set up. Here again is an example of the level of commitment that is required from child-centered teachers.

When you begin showing up to school a bit earlier than usual, but really do not see the value of preparing the environment prior to the children's arrival, or if you view arriving early as simply "adding an extra hour to my day," or "I don't get paid for it, why show up?" your new behavior will not last because the commitment level is not yet there. You may do it for a day or two, possibly a week, but if you ultimately do not understand the WHY behind the action; you will not continue the new behavior.

Preparing the environment and getting it ready is an investment that pays dividends later in the day. You reap the benefits as you realize and internalize the importance of calmer, smoother, better prepared mornings. Having the environment ready for the children AS SOON AS THEY ARRIVE will eliminate many behavior problems. Make a commitment to get to school earlier than the children and prepare the room and activities. Then, you will be able to stop spending the mornings running around like a chicken with your head cut off hollering "Wait stop!! Stop! That's CLOSED! It's not time for that yet!"

Now, onto the second point – the rules you are attempting to enforce. Children need to be able to explore with few restrictions, but this does not mean NO rules! It means we must own up to the fact that most rules within a preschool serve no purpose other than allowing adults to remain in control of children. These are the kinds of rules and restrictions we should take an honest look at. We need to question the rules and ask ourselves, "Are my expectations of preschoolers in line with what they are capable of developmentally?" and, "Whose needs are being met with these rules?"

Watch me climb!

It is essential that we question whether or not our expectations of children are age appropriate. Children cannot sit still, be quiet or use walking feet. When we expect things from two, three and four year olds that they are not ready to do, we are setting everyone up for frustration, power struggles and conflict.

29

The time you spend examining your rules, expectations and in setting up your environment before the children arrive, is an investment that pays off all day. With this simple investment, you do not have to say NO NO NO NO all day long. You can say YES a lot more because you have already done the work. The environment is engaging, exciting and welcoming. As soon as the children come in they can begin exploring.

Identifying Characteristic #3
ADULTS ACTING AS FACILITATORS

The process of becoming a facilitator is a journey of self-awareness. If you look up "facilitate" in the dictionary it says: "to make easier." Are we facilitating? Or hindering and hovering? Do we view education as the filling of a bucket, or the lighting of a fire?

Ask yourself, "Am I the keeper of the stuff?" Am I the keeper of the playdough, the keeper of the "good" books? Do you (literally or figuratively) wear a key around your neck that opens the cupboard in which all of the markers, glue, paint, paper, shaker bottles, animal figures, chalk are kept?

I told you earlier how in my early days of teaching, I was paired up with a teacher who had a masking tape line-up line in the center of the room. She also had laminated lesson plans, a whistle and a timer. She was not a facilitator. She viewed herself as the keeper of the knowledge and her role as "teacher" was to fill the children with this knowledge. The key she wore around her neck opened the cupboard containing the materials children needed: chalk, paint, crayons, and clay. She was, quite literally, the keeper of the stuff.

Being able to engage in activities within this room was a challenge for everyone because we (myself included) had to ASK for everything. If she was in a bad mood, or just didn't want to bother or (god forbid) if we had already colored that morning, she would say, "No, we aren't getting the crayons out now." This is not facilitating.

Now, here's the scary part, an example of the power of modeling, and how actions speak louder than words - even though I didn't like the behaviors I saw, I adopted some of them in my early years of teaching. I had rigid lesson plans, a schedule we followed to the minute, I said NO a lot, did tons of cut-out patterned art and even had masking tape line-up lines. I also had HUGE laminated STOP signs. When I did not want one of the classroom centers opened, or did not want a particular area available to the children, I would hang up the STOP sign. The STOP sign meant that the center was CLOSED, and I took great pride in the fact that I was teaching the kids how to read STOP (Arrugh).

If it was 4:30 on a Friday afternoon (and I left at 5:00) and I had already put the paint and paper away, or, had already washed the paint cups and brushes, the easel would be CLOSED. If I had a headache and didn't want to listen to the sounds of crashing wooden blocks on the tile floor, the block center would be CLOSED. If I was sick of listening to who was going to wear the blue click-click high heel shoes, or who gets the doctor coat, or who was the baby kitty last time, the dress-up area would be CLOSED. See the pattern?

This was not facilitating. MY needs were being met, not those of the children. Do you think I had behavior problems with the children who wanted to paint, build or play dress-up?? YOU BET! Was that my own fault? YOU BET! Did I give myself permission to rethink what I was doing, change my mind, throw the signs away and get over it? YOU BET! Did it happen over night?? NO WAY! But when it did, the main reason it worked was because I believed in why I was taking the STOP signs down. If I had tried to make changes too soon, it probably would not have worked because I wasn't ready yet. Remember the power of baby steps. Give yourself permission to change your mind. Question everything you do. We must think about what we are doing and saying in the classroom. We must be aware of the messages we send, we cannot simply flip on automatic auto-pilot, going through the motions doing the same things we've always done year after year since 1985.

I NEED SOME MORE BAGS!

One morning we had shaving cream, ziploc bags, watercolors and pipettes out on the art table. Shaving cream had been a consistent and regular part of our routine, so I did not need to be hovering over the children who were exploring the shaving cream. Rachel was at the art table; she squirted some shaving cream into the bag, added some (I assume) yellow and blue watercolors, closed her bag and began to squish the bag. All of a sudden I heard this squeal of glee and excitement, "Ms. Lisa," she yelled, "Ms. Lisa, I made green!" I jumped up and went over to the table, "Yes you did! What else do you need?" She looked up at me with her big brown eyes and said plainly and matter of factly, "I need some more bags."

I went to the cupboard, brought her a whole box of ziplocs. She made forty of them, squirting, mixing, and squishing each of them, excitedly yelling after each one, "Ms. Lisa, I did it again!" and "Ms. Lisa, I AM STILL making green!"

Early in my teaching (before I new better) I would have quizzed Rachel, probing to find out what colors she used: as if that mattered. I would have asked her to regurgitate back to me HOW she did it and would've convinced myself that I had taught her how to make green. The freedom of exploration would not have been there because back then, I was the keeper of the stuff, the monitor of the baggies and the squirter of the shaving cream.

A big part of my journey has been learning the art of becoming a facilitator, learning how to "teach" less and share more. Over the years I have learned the value of providing the time and materials necessary for children to come to their own conclusions and make their own discoveries. It's not about teaching them green. Rachel went on to Kindergarten knowing how to identify green and knowing how to make green, but not because I had "Green Week" at the preschool. And she most definitely did not learn it because I said, "Wear a green shirt tomorrow!!" Rachel learned about green because she was in an environment that gave her the time and materials she needed to make some connections between yellow, blue, cause, effect, action, reaction and colors.

Encouraging children to make connections like Rachel's is a major part of facilitating. Child-centered teachers realize that what might look like "just playing" to an observer, is usually about any or all of the following: science, observation, action, reaction, cause and effect, gravity, density, absorption, evaporation, colors, vibrations, saturation point, surface tension, spatial representation, weight, volume, distance, balance, rhythm or physics. It is our responsibility as educators to facilitate experiences that are meaningful to children; experiences that are ultimately linked to concepts they'll be exposed to later on in their education. Our job now is to connect the experiences to the concepts in a manner that allows the children to be actively involved in their explorations and discoveries about the world around them.

Identifying Characteristic #4
LOTS OF OUTDOOR TIME

Tree climbing

Children NEED, and MUST have, a lot of time out of doors. Although in our society outside time is often seen as wasted time, we cannot allow this incorrect mindset to continue. The Alliance for Childhood is a partnership of individuals and organizations committed to fostering and respecting each child's inherent right to a healthy, developmentally appropriate childhood. In the fall of 2000 they reported that a recent survey indicated that 40 percent of our schools have considered eliminating recess!

Parks and playgrounds are being leveled for shopping malls while many of the ones that remain, although saved from the bulldozer, are being stripped of those "dangerous" things known as slides and swings.

When I do my "Let's Go Outside" workshop I ask participants, "What games did you play when you were little?" and "Where did you play?" I never cease to be amazed at the power of these two simple questions. They encourage discussions and generate the recollection of memories, some forgotten ones, some favorite ones, and the questions solicit similar answers in all the groups I've worked with, "I played outside," "I remember being always with a lot of other children," "In fields," "In rivers," "Play forts and tree houses," "Vacant lots" and "Construction sites." No one really remembers a lot of adults hovering around and most remember all the neighborhood children playing together (even threes, fours and fives all in the same group - imagine that!).

Do you remember being told to "come home when the street lights come on?" Or to "be home in time for lunch?" When I think about the long hours children are spending in day care, safety concerns that discourage parents from freely saying, "go play outside," the shortening (or complete elimination) of recess, the tendency to replace natural wooded play areas with strip malls and parking lots and the inappropriate mindset of many American's that outside time is wasted time, I worry that many of today's children will not have similar memories when they are older.

However, instead of lamenting this thought, I encourage preschool teachers and child care providers to start viewing their playgrounds, parks and backyards as places where they can recreate what children and families used to have in their own neighborhoods. Luther Burbank (1849-1926), the world's foremost plant breeder, friend to Helen Keller, Henry Ford and Thomas Edison and creative inspiration to many painters, sculptors and writers said, "Every child should have mud pies, grasshoppers, tadpoles, frogs, acorns, wild strawberries, trees to climb, brooks to wade, animals to pet, pine cones, rocks to roll, sand, snakes, huckleberries and hornets; any child who has been deprived of these has been deprived of the best part of his/her education." (This quote was shared by Lori Schoen and Tina Springmeyer during their workshop, "Making the Most of your Outdoor Environment", presented at the California Kindergarten Conference, January, 1999.)

We must make sure that children have ample time to play outside. To wallow in the mud, sand and water, with enough time to poke things in the dirt, catch rollie pollies and frogs and roll down hills. We need to resist the urge to fill our yards and classrooms with the newest, latest, greatest thing from the new school supply catalogs. Instead, remember that children enjoy and NEED loose parts that they can haul around: pvc pipe, tires, gutter, old kitchen tools, buckets, spools, cups, wooden planks, milk crates, carpet squares and carpet tubing, funnels and shovels. We can also come to realize the importance of taking other things outside such as the easel, blocks, books, water table tubs. All of the goodies we think of as "inside things" could, would, and should be outside too.

The outdoor environment is more conducive to the active learning style of preschoolers. Large motor muscles of arms and legs that encourage running, jumping and climbing, all need to be given enough time to develop. This has to happen before the quiet, small motor muscles for holding pens and pencils can do their jobs appropriately. Some children love to run around all day, and would stay outside all day if they were allowed to. I think this is great. At our school we sometimes stay out all day, coming inside to get cleaned up or to nap, but usually playing outside all day, even eating out under the big tree.

It is a rare instance when children holler, "I wanna go in, I wanna go in!" More often than not they clamor at your ankles all morning wondering, "When it is time to go out??" In her book *The Great Outdoors: Restoring a Child's Right to Play Outside,* author Mary Rivkin tells us that what grown ups might consider "cozy" can quickly turn into "cooped up" when you are three.

Spools are excellent loose parts

Bring your easels outside! The ball, ropes, swings and buckets too. Make a garden, and even a mud pit. The children will learn about balance as they attempt to build block castles on the lawn's bumpy uneven surface. They will learn about evaporation while painting with tin cans, water and brushes all over the patio, wondering aloud, "where did the water go?" They'll experience cause and effect as they dump pinecones into a tub of water and witness an amazing transformation. They'll learn about absorption by making tie-dye shirts every summer wondering how the color stays on the shirts.

Mary Rivkin goes on to inform us that "firsthand experiences in the natural world are valuable, perhaps crucial…a lot of learning goes on outside, but when children are always inside they miss out on such experiences." Begin viewing the outdoor space as an extension of your classroom, not separate from it. Outside time is not wasted time.

Have water available everyday!

Making Time For Change
CONTINUING THE JOURNEY

Becoming child-centered is being willing to grow, willing to think about the things we do and being willing to change. Change takes time. We are creatures of habit and often don't honor the amount of time needed to make necessary changes. Knowing this, Vancouver based child development expert, Jenny Chapman, assists teachers and child care providers through the cycle of change by encouraging them through the steps listed below. This cycle of change was developed and shared by Jenny at the 1999 Good Stuff for Kids Conference and is used with her permission.

1. Identify the issue to be changed (ie: using coloring books, cutting out patterns for art, etc.)

2. Observe and identify another practice (open ended art)

3. Reflect and commit to change

4. Make an attempt to implement the change and form a new habit

5. Push through fear and frustration of putting a new idea into practice

6. Be aware of resistance

7. Repeat the new behavior

8. Create a new habit and pattern

9. Evaluate and Refine

10. The new behavior or practice is now imprinted. Now apply the same process to other issues to be changed.

We must be gentle with ourselves while seriously thinking about what we do. We MUST give ourselves permission to change our minds as we travel on our journey. I have developed what I call the 3E's to serve as three main guideposts as we continue our journey of becoming more child-centered.

The 3E's are Ego, Environment and Experiences. It is through an in-depth exploration of these ideas that we become stronger, more focused and able to develop a deeper understanding of what it means to truly be child-centered.

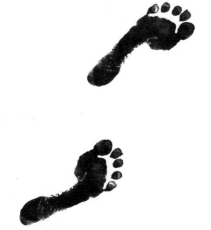

EGO
What if today was their only day?

It is vital that while we are on our journey of becoming more child-centered we take time to examine our own egos and our own control issues. Early childhood expert Bev Bos stated that, "in order for the lives of our children to be optimal, the adults in the world must be less egocentric than the children."

We must determine if we are establishing control with and for children, or over them. We must remember the power in controlling the environment and not the little people in it. I know individuals who went into teaching because they enjoy telling people who are smaller than them what to do. We must ask ourselves, "Why am I in this field?" and we must examine the things we may bring into the classroom that serve as stumbling blocks and speed bumps on our journey of personal and professional growth.

The best way to get a handle on some of the controlling behaviors you may bring into the classroom is to tape-record yourself as you interact with the children during the day. I did this early on in my teaching, and recently found the tapes again. WOW! Such evidence of growth! Remember change takes time and doesn't happen over night. Taping allows you to document where you are at *now* so someday you will be able to see how far you've come!

I continue to keep my control issues in balance by always asking myself, "What if today was their only day?" If today, Monday or Wednesday was this child's only experience in an early childhood educational environment, and they were spending it with me, what will they take with them? What will they remember? What will their memory of this place, this day, and me, be?

Will it be, "don't," "stop," "because I said so," "get back on your nap mat," "lunch is over," "get out of the bathroom," "wait," "sit still," "be quiet," "I'm waiting," "how many times do I have to tell you." Or. . . . . "do you want to read that story again?" "do you need some more paper?," "do you need a few more bags?," "who needs anything?," "what else can I get you?" "would you like to hold the hose?" "want to pour your juice yourself?" "let's see what happens."

I believe that examining our ego is the hardest and most difficult part of the journey. It takes a great deal of commitment to realize that in order to be excellent we must take an in-depth look at our ego and our control issues. We know we impact the lives of the children we work with. It takes great strength and confidence to identify areas in need of improvement and to do what's necessary to be the best we can be.

ENVIRONMENT

Does it reflect the people who spend the most time in it?

There are two parts to this "E"; logistical and philosophical. Logistically, you need to make sure you have enough of the ingredients that make up a childcare setting. Some of the major ingredients are things like flour, glue, water, cream of tartar, corn starch, bubbles, vinegar, baking soda, paint, glue, scissors, tape, paper, buckets, shovels and books. I would venture so far as to say that the latest, brightest, shiniest new thing from one of the many school supply catalogs is NOT something you need. But the catalogs can be tempting. I used to spend half my paycheck on "stuff" for the children. I changed my mind though, and now use a lot of recycled and natural materials, avoiding anything plastic as often as possible.

I know a teacher who was given a ream of 8 ½ x 11 typing paper and told it was to last 6 months. Meanwhile, there was a new $10,000 climbing structure out on the yard that none of the children could use because it was too big. It was designed for elementary, NOT preschool children. Paper, not a climbing structure, is an essential ingredient for a preschool. Granted, as a business owner I realize that clean, shiny, sturdy equipment on the playground attracts potential clients, which in turn keeps new children enrolling and subsequently affords me job security, but at the expense of what? How many times have you found the hoarded gallon of glue in your co-teachers cabinet? How much time has been wasted hunting down the tape, scissors or yellow paint? Have you ever been guilty of hiding the contraband glitter in your backpack? Just like the children who stuff playdough in their pockets because they don't know when it will be out of the cupboard again, teachers who are not provided the ingredients essential to the business of working with children, become frustrated at the inconsistency and absence of the materials they need to do their job.

If you are licensed for 108 children and have only four bikes on the playground, you are going to have behavioral problems. If you have twenty-four children in your room and only one sensory tub, you will struggle with the same issue. If you are licensed for six and only have one toy dump truck, you will have a similar reaction. These are logistical things we need to examine as we are setting up our environment. Don't get me wrong; I am not an advocate of children having (or needing) a lot of stuff. I personally believe that open ended loose parts such as tires, shovels, buckets, PVC pipe and other open-ended materials the kids can drag around are best. I am not a proponent of single purpose toys and am a firm believer that the more creative the toy the less creative the child needs to be. I am in agreement with Ferenc Mate who, in his book, *A Reasonable Life: Toward a Simpler, Secure, More Humane Existence*, states, "Most child psychologists agree that every time we give a child a toy we prevent him from inventing it." My point is that there are ingredients that are central to our jobs; make sure you have enough of them.

Philosophically, we must look around our playroom or school, and ask, "Does this environment reflect the people who spend the most time in it?" If an outsider walked into your room would they know that the children were the A-1 priority?

Are there photos of the children, their families, their pets, and their friends on the walls where the children can view them? Are the bulletin boards displaying art low enough where children can see the pictures? Or are the boards up high serving as a parent pleaser?

Some children spend anywhere from six, to ten, to twelve hours in child care environments. Are they able to move freely within the environment with time for both active and calm play? Or, is there pressure to always be "busy doing" all day long. Children need to have cozy corners, nooks and crannies where they can hide out. Throw a sheet over a table and toss some pillows under there too. Don't just do this on a rainy day. Have it available all the time. Section off an area where the children can be lazy with a doll, teddy bear, blanket and/or book; they need time and space to "tune-out" when in the same place for a long time.

Examine whether or not your environment allows for appropriate risk taking experiences. In the National Education Association's publication of *Play's Place in Public Education for Young Children,* we learn that risk taking is linked to literacy. In their article, "Play, Risk Taking and the Emergence of Literacy," contained within the above mentioned book, authors Ann Fordham and William Anderson state, "Children who are afraid to risk rarely become fluent readers. They shrink from the venturesome activity that is essential for literacy to flourish. Forced attention to an intricate set of unreliable and confusing rules takes precedence over natural tendencies to explore."

Children need to jump off things and climb on things. Of course they are doing this while you are watching them. You must not be chatting with your co-teachers about your favorite TV show while the kids are jumping off the big boulder!

Children who do not risk when they are little grow up looking for risks to take when they are older. But when you are twenty-nine years old, sliding down a slide, face first, butt naked into a mud puddle doesn't really meet the risk requirement it might have when you were four. So what do you do? Drive 125 miles an hour down the freeway? Bungee jump? Climb to the top of an elevator and try to get off before it hits the top of the building? Commonly called "elevator surfing," it is the current "risk" of choice for some young people. I'd rather assist in cleaning up a skinned knee or helping rinse out a mouthful of sand then get a call from the police at 2:00 am asking me to identify my teenager.

Now, I am in NO WAY encouraging you to compromise safety. What I am encouraging you to do is realize the importance of behaviors such as: climbing UP slides, swinging on tummies, jumping off swings, spider swinging (two children swinging together while facing each other), climbing up and jumping off rocks, hanging from the monkey bars and dropping into the sand below and even having two children on the bike at one time. Ask yourself "what is the worse possible thing that could happen?" And then examine your answer. A mouthful of sand? A skinned knee? A tumble? Is it really that bad and dangerous? Or is it easier to just say NO?

Walk around your room or space and question whether or not you would feel welcomed within these walls if you were two? three? four? Do the children feel like they belong there? The banner over my door said, "This is a child's place and we move at a child's pace." Is your space a "child's place," or does it just say that on the informational brochure? If today was their only day what would their memory of the space be?

What does your environment smell like? Many centers I visit smell and look like over-sanitized doctor's offices. What smells permeate the rooms of your school? Bleach? Simple Green? Pine-Sol? Our sense of smell is our strongest link to memory; knowing this, plant scented flowers, burn incense, have potpourri in baskets around the room, put vanilla on the light bulbs and let cinnamon sticks and water simmer on the stove. You want these smells within the environment so that as the children grow up they will associate these pleasant smells with preschool and their time with you. I want my children to remember me, and their time with me, when they experience pleasant smells like cookies baking and apples simmering on the stove, not when they walk down the janitorial aisle at the grocery store.

Walk around your room tomorrow morning and get down on the floor, what does it smell like down there? What does it look like? Crawl around your environment on your hands and knees. Would you want to be three, four or five and playing on the floor down there? Do you like what you experience in your room when you make yourself their size? Is it pleasant? Homey? Cozy? Calm? Engaging? If not figure out what you need to do and take that first baby step to change.

EXPERIENCES
Down With Dittos

Children need to be engaged in experiences that are meaningful to them. The challenge is that sometimes what is meaningful to children is NOT what is meaningful to adults. Like when Michelle played for an hour with the box the easel came in by sliding back and forth over the smooth surface on her tummy, never once asking to take the easel out of the box. Or, when Ryan stood for fifteen minutes shaking the slinky that was suspended from the ceiling, up and down and up and down! Or, when Jasmin spent ten minutes spinning and spinning in the middle of the room and her mom said, "Come on, it's time to go," to which she replied, "Hold on, I'm almost done," and started to spin in the opposite direction.

As adults, we sometimes forget the fun of empty boxes, slinkies and spinning in circles. As concerned parents or teachers we might look at behaviors like these and ask, *"What are they doing?"* Let me reassure you that, in actuality, they are doing a lot - we have just forgotten. It may serve us well to consider removing our "grown-up glasses" as we observe children at play and allow ourselves to remember the magic of being little and the power and pleasure of such experiences.

In her book, *Endangered Minds Why Children Don't Think and What We Can Do About It*, author Jane Healy reminds us that children need experiences to attach words to. Preschool children need ample opportunity to connect concepts to experiences. Taking the time to link concepts with experiences is one example of the higher level of dedication and commitment evidenced in child-centered teachers. You will see these instructors link the concept of absorption to the experience of using eyedroppers to drip-drop colored water onto cotton balls. They will link the concept of gravity to the experience of jumping off rocks, swings and chairs. They link the concept of evaporation to the experience of painting the sidewalk with a tin can filled with water, wondering where the water went. These experiences are structured and organized. Child-centered teachers are keen observers, aware of the research in their field and of why they do what they do. The only thing they have given up is the need to have control over the children. These teachers have embraced a child-initiated model of learning and work to create environments that emphasize the importance of social and emotional skills, rather than academics, in the early years. Recent studies point out that preschoolers in environments that stress social and emotional development do better in school than preschoolers who were doing dittos, ABCs and 123s.

In her article, "How Do Your Children Grow?" (Executive Educator, 1995) author Susan Black provides an overview of the work of Rebecca Marcon, a developmental psychologist and professor of psychology at the University of North Florida in Jacksonville. Marcon had been asked to investigate the high rates of retention within Washington D.C's early grades. Marcon sorted the district's preschool programs into three categories, the child-initiated model, the academically directed model and the "middle of the road" (borrowing features from the other two) model. Her studies conclusively show that only the children in the child-initiated preschools benefited from their early preschool experience. By age nine, children who had been in preschools that stressed academics were earning lower grades and passing fewer reading and math objectives. By age eleven these same children were behind their peers developmentally and displaying maladaptive behaviors such as depression, hyperactivity, anxiety and defiance.

And, in September 2000, a report released by the Child Mental Health Foundations and Agencies Network entitled "A Good Beginning: Sending America's Children to School with the Social and Emotional Competence They Need to Succeed," readers learn that being ready for school means being friendly, attentive and curious. Failing to instill these qualities during the preschool years sets children up for failure.

Every day preschool children need to be creating, moving, singing, discussing, observing, reading and playing. *Sitting still and being quiet is not a marketable job skill.* We must not put emphasis on passive learning. In *Endangered Minds,* author Jane Healy reminds us that in years past, children had experiences. They were taken places, and spoken to not at. She laments that "what now constitutes an experience is to go buy a workbook." She reminds us that, "without experiences there are no concepts and with no concepts there is no attention span because they (the children) don't know what you're talking about."

What does this mean? It means that, in the words of Jane Healy, children need experiences to attach words to! Will you be talking about apples the first week of school? Bring in real ones - dozens of them! Red ones, green ones, yellow ones too! Cut them, smell them, taste them, make applesauce, decide who likes which kind best, paint with apples and plant the seeds. Connect meaningful, hands-on experiences to the concept of apple. Do this with ANY theme, project, topic or concept that is brought into the classroom. Talking about pumpkins? Bring in real ones, carve them, put the squishy insides into the sensory tub, paint with the stem part, make pie and toast the seeds. Talking about trees? Go out and hug real ones, take bark rubbings, sit and read under them, climb them and chalk trace their shadows. I go so far as to say that if you cannot bring them to it, or it to them ("it" being the concept or the idea) it probably doesn't belong in a preschool classroom.

It is our job to create places where children are engaged in experiences that are meaningful, where they can connect concepts to experiences, and where language can be developed because they are attaching words to their experiences. We must make sure we are not just planning and setting out the various, cute, new, novel, random activities we just gathered up at the weekend's conference.

Experience is the foundation that supports the house of higher learning. Stay strong against the pressure to start building that house of academics where there is no foundation. What happens if you build a house with no foundation? It falls down! What happens when we push academics to soon?

Preschool children do not need bite-sized morsels of an elementary school curriculum. Provide them with long periods of free time, facilitate their explorations, examine your rules and encourage lots of outdoor playtime.

In his book, *Evolution's End: Claiming the Potential of Our Intelligence*, author Joseph Chilton Pearce tells us that, "Little learning comes from forced willful attempts to 'make' children learn, give them caring adults, ample materials, lots of time in an environment filled with rich engaging experiences and you cannot prevent the brain from learning, because learning is what it is designed to do."

THREE FLAT CIRCLES!

One December in San Diego I was teamed up with a preschool teacher who was planning two weeks of curriculum based around the theme of "winter." One day she made a big batch of white clay, intending for the children to make snowmen. She distributed a tray and some clay to each child saying, "Today we are making snowmen!" ONE child out of the eighteen in the room made three balls, piled them on top of each other and declared his snowman finished, the rest took three balls of clay and squished them flat onto the tray. The teacher got very frustrated – they didn't look like snowmen! They looked like pancakes! How could the kids take them home for their holiday art?

Remember my own glue bottle and paper pumpkin fiasco?? Sensing her frustration, I allowed myself to remember my own frantic behavior the day those children didn't do that project "right" either. That chaotic day of preparing, cutting and begging seemed so long ago. I felt confident that I was on the path of becoming more child-centered and this allowed me to wonder . . . Might I be ready? Could I be her Cynde?

I decided to take the risk. I thought about what I would say. What *should* I say? Should I even say anything? How will my words be received? I didn't know. I was nervous. I wondered if Cynde had been nervous. I took a deep breath and stood up calmly, like Cynde. I was still thinking about what I would say as I glanced casually around the room and over to her bookshelf.

What would I say? Then, still looking at the bookshelf, I noticed something –
something similar about all the books on the "winter" themed bookshelf.

I slowly walked over to the books, and as I picked one up, I softly asked the
air, "When you grow up in San Diego, and your only experience of a
snowman is in a book. . . what does it look like?"

She stopped. She looked at me, then at the book. I didn't know what to do or
say. She glanced at the book again. Then she smiled. Looking back at me, still
smiling, she softly said, "three flat circles."

She took her first step into a larger world.

I wish you strength, courage and success as you do the same.

Cornstarch + Water = Ooblick!

OOEY GOOEY
Activities

MONOPRINTS

You Need: Paint
Paper
A table you can easily wipe off

Directions:

Put some paint directly on a table. Allow the children to fingerpaint on the table. When they are finished, let them put a piece of paper on top of their fingerpainting, press it flat, and lift it up. It will take a print the fingerprint design they made on the table.

Clean up:

Use sponges and squeegees to clean up. Allow the kids to help too!

Suggestion:

Toddlers can do this one right at the high chair!

Color Mixing

Small Motor Skills

Stages of Scribbling

Creativity

Print Making

COZY SPOTS

You Need: Tables with sheets over them
Cardboard boxes
Pillows and old sheets
A squared off corner

Directions:

Use available objects and materials to assist you in creating a cozy spot, nook or cranny for the children within your environment. The children will often times create them themselves. Allow them.

Helpful Hint:

Don't save these forts and secret hiding spots for rainy days! Have cozy spots available for the children all the time. Solicit ideas and suggestions from the children too!

Our book area is by an old wooden crate. The crate is filled with pillows and covered with an old quilt. Quite cozy indeed!

SWINGING ON YOUR TUMMY PAINTING

You Need: Swings

Paper (a long sheet of mural or butcher works best here)

Paint

Paint cups

Brushes

Directions:

Lay the paper under the swing. Put the paint cups and brushes close by. Allow the children to swing on their tummies and paint at the same time!

Even teachers get into the action!

Large and Small Motor Development

Pre-writing, Creativity

Coordination and Balance

60

PUDDING PAINTING

You Need: Pudding
Paper (fingerpaint paper works best)
Cups and spoons

Directions:

Make a batch of pudding. Give each child a cup filled with pudding and a spoon.
Let them scoop the pudding onto their paper and fingerpaint with it.

Helpful Hint:

Some will paint with the pudding, some will eat the pudding, some will paint
with their fingers and some will paint with the spoon!

Creativity

Sensory Awareness

Stages of Scribbling

Small Motor Development

WINDOW PAINTING

Hand-Eye Coordination

Large Motor Development (Those Big Swooping Arm Movements)

Small Motor

Color Mixing

Spatial Awareness (Where am I Putting the Scribbles and Marks?)

Creativity

You Need: A sliding glass door or a low window

Paint

Paint cups

Brushes

Directions:

Allow the children to paint on the window or the door! Handprints are especially fun. Children can be on both sides of the window so that it looks like they are painting on each other!

Clean Up:

When you are ready to clean off the windows, spray the painted area with squirt bottles or with the hose to get it wet. Then use a scrubber sponge to clean off the paint. The kids love to help too!

OBJECT ART

You Need: Many varied items to make prints with.
My favorites include:
Legos
Duplos
Bath puffs
Corks
Cotton balls
Apples
Kitchen utensils
Plungers
Carrot tops
Strawberry baskets
Paper plate of paint
Butcher or Mural paper

Plunger Prints!

Directions:

Cover a long table with the paper. Place the printing materials and the paint on the paper. Allow the kids to explore and print with the various objects.

Creativity, Exploration, Small Motor Development,
Self Expression, "Out-of-The-Box" Thinking and Inquiry (What
Else Can I Do With this?!)

MARBLE PAINTING

You Need: A box

Paint

Marbles

Paper

Hand-Eye Coordination

Tracking (Watching the Marbles go Back and Forth)

Creativity

Color Mixing

Focusing

Directions:

Put some paper in the marble painting box. Allow the children to spoon or squirt some paint on top of the paper. Drop in some marbles! Rock the box back and forth back and forth!

Suggestion:

This is one of the staples of preschool art. Kids can do it all week long! Let them! Let the boxes dry and reuse them over and over. My marble painting boxes are almost 10 years old!

Variations:

Try the same project with KOOSH BALLS and even GOLF BALLS!

STRAW BLOWING ART

You Need: Liquid watercolors

Paper

Turkey basters or pipettes (basters are great for smaller hands)

Straws

Directions:

Using the pipettes or basters, drip-drop the liquid watercolor paint onto the paper. Use the straws to blow the paint in all directions! Twist and turn the paper to make the paint run and drip in many different directions. You can even just use your mouth to blow really hard if the straws are awkward for the kids.

Movement of Air (Blowing)

Action And Reaction
(Blow-Get a Splot)

Creativity

Color Mixing

SQUIRT BOTTLE ART

Squeezing of the Bottle Assists in Hand Strength (Pre-Writing)

Negative/ Positive Space

Matching

Creativity

You Need: Squirt bottles that preschool sized hands can hold

Paper

Liquid watercolor paints

Directions:

Use the liquid watercolor to color the water in the squirt bottles. Tape paper to the easel, the ground, a table or a wall. Allow the children to squirt the paper!!

Variations:

After taping the paper down, put nature items such as leaves, rocks, grass, even your hand on the paper. Squirt the object with the colored water! Watch the print that's left behind.

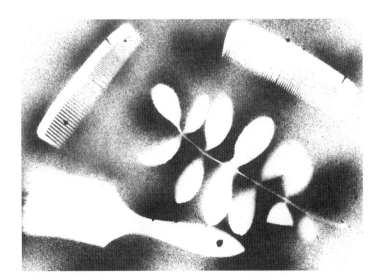

SAND GLUING

You Need: Sand from the beach or your playground

Powdered tempra paint (optional)

Paper plate "dump" plate

Glue

Heavy Paper or even cardboard

(I save the back page from paper tablets for this activity!)

Exploration of Line and Design

Color Mixing

Creativity

Squeezing the Glue Bottle
Facilitates Hand Strength
(Pre-writing)

Directions:

Allow the kids to make squiggly glue designs on the heavy paper and then sprinkle their sand over their glue. Dump the extra off onto the "dump" plates that you have placed around the table. Mix powdered tempra with the sand to make your sand many colors!

RAINY DAY ART

Weather Investigation

Creativity

Seasons

Action/Reaction
(Powder to Paint)

Cause/Effect
(Rain + Paint=Picture)

You Need: A rainy day

Dry powdered tempra (in a shaker bottle is best)

Heavy easel paper

Directions:

Shake some colored powdered tempra onto the paper. If you don't have a shaker bottle use a spoon and sprinkle some on. Let them use as many colors as they want. Walk onto the playground and put it in the rain! Stand by and watch what happens!

Variation:

Uh-oh!!?? No rain today??? Use the same process, but allow the children to squirt their paper with a spray bottle filled with water, set on mist setting. Or even stand over the paper and drip drop water drops using pipettes or eyedroppers.

BUBBLE JUICE SOLUTION

You Need: Dawn dishwashing soap
Water

Bubble blowing with straws.

Directions:

The basic formula is 6 cups water to 2 cups Dawn. Increase or decrease the formula depending on how much you need. Blow bubbles with toilet paper tubes, berry baskets, 6-pak rings, the trays that flowers come in, PVC pipe, straws and even your hands!

Helpful hints:

1. Clean up spills with a mixture of vinegar and water.
2. If your bubbles are popping too soon – add more soap.

Popping bubbles that landed on the lawn!

Air Explorations

Surface Tension (When will it POP!?)

Question and Inquiry (Why are Overcast Days Better than Hot Ones for Bubbles?)

69

ICE CUBE PAINTING

You Need: Ice cube trays
Liquid watercolor paint
Paper
Popsicle sticks

Properties of Water
(Liquid—Solid—Liquid)

Color Mixing

Small Motor

Creativity

Temperature

Freezing/Melting

Directions:

Fill the ice cube tray 2/3 full of water. Fill the remaining space with the liquid watercolor paint. Freeze. After the ice cubes have frozen, let the kids zoom the colored ice cubes around their paper to make ice tracks! Some kids will want to push the ice with their fingers; some will want to use Popsicle sticks.

NYLON SPLAT ART

You Need: Knee-hi's filled with sand or popcorn kernels and tied off in a knot

Big sheets of paper

Newspaper to cover the floor (if you do it inside)

Trays of paint

Gravity

Socialization

Color Mixing

Creativity

Force

Judging Distance and
Estimating Results
(How High for Best Splat?
How High for Loudest Splat?
Where will it Land if I Move
Over a Little Bit?)

Directions:

Fill the knee-hi's 1/3 full with sand or un-popped popcorn kernels. Tie a knot in the top so the popcorn or sand doesn't fall out. Allow the children to position themselves on chairs with their paper on the floor in front of them. Dip dip the nylon splatters into some paint, hold it way up high and let it drop - splat! - down onto their paper.

Variation:

Bring it outside! Allow the kids to stand at the top of the slide or the climbing structure using the railing for support. Put the paper down on the sand and have them send their nylon spatters down to the paper below!

TENNIS BALL BOUNCE

Large Motor (Throwing the Ball)

Creativity

Color Mixing

Force

Speed

Velocity

Tracking

Observations
(Hey! The Ball Came Back!)

You Need: A big sheet that can get painty!

Tennis balls

Trays of paint

Directions:

This is an outside favorite of mine. Drag the sheet in the sand and secure each corner with a pile of sand, or some small rocks – you don't want it blowing away. Allow the kids to dip the balls into the paint and toss the balls around on the sheet.

Remember:

Some kids will hurl the balls - most toss them around. You can have sheets of paper to capture the "art" to bring home – all the while remembering the importance of process – not product!

Variation:

Instead of a sheet, tape a long piece of paper down to the ground either inside or outside. Allow the kids to roll the painty tennis balls down the paper! This is always a favorite too.

CAR TRACKS

You Need: Plastic cars – the bigger the better – I often use Lego cars

Trays of paint

Long sheets of paper

Directions:

Put the paper around the table or even on the floor, or even outside on the playground. Allow the children to dip the cars into paint and make car tracks all over their paper.

Helpful Hint:

Some kids will paint with the cars for one minute and then will proceed to make a fingerpainting. That's OK! Remember we are focusing on the process, and the child's creativity, not what was on our lesson plan book! When I use the lego cars, often times the kids will take the lego cars apart and proceed to make lego prints – that's OK too!

Tracking (Eyes Following the Zooming Cars)

Dramatic Play

Creativity

Small Motor

CLEAN MUD

You Need: Bars of Ivory Soap
Old cheese graters
Water table or sensory tub
Toilet paper
Pitcher of water

Directions:

In a sensory tub mix together about 4 bars of grated soap, toilet paper and a pitcher full of water. Squish and squish until it looks like soapy sudsy cool-whip! There is no real "recipe." Just keep adding more until it feels soft, soapy and creamy! If it gets stiff and dry, reconstitute with more hot water. Dispose of Clean Mud in the trash NOT down the drain! I leave it out for a few days before disposing of it. Just keep adding more of the ingredients! Watch for allergies to the soap!

Small Motor (Squeezing and Squishing Facilitate Hand Strength)
Cause/Effect (Soap + Water + TP = Goo!)
Practical Skills (Grating)
Sensory and Tactile Awareness

KITCHEN BRUSH MURALS

You Need: A random assortment of kitchen, bathroom and miscellaneous brushes such as baby bottle brushes, kitchen dish brushes, BBQ brushes, sponge brushes, toilet brushes and scrubbers.

Trays of paint
Mural or butcher paper

Large and Small Motor Development

Printing

Creativity

Questioning/Inquiry (What Else Can I Do With This?)

Directions:

Allow the children to paint and explore the designs made by the assorted brushes. You can use these brushes to paint at the easel too!

Suggestion:

Ask the milkman to donate a milk crate to store the many brushes in. This way they are available whenever anyone wants to check them out! Send the milkman a thank you note along with a photo of how you used the crates!

TOOTHBRUSH PAINTING

You Need: Old toothbrushes

Paper

Paint

Small Motor

Creativity

Directions:

Set up your art area to allow free exploration of the materials.

A Few Suggestions:

Resist the urge to cut the paper into the shape of a tooth to make it look as though the kids "learned" something today!! Save all of your old toothbrushes, bleach them, and then put them in your art box. Change out your easel brushes and replace with toothbrushes for a few days and see what happens!

Helpful Hint:

If your preschool (like my first one) is in a strip mall location where there IS a dentist or an orthodontist, walk over and visit. Request some toothbrushes for your project. Follow up with a thank you and a picture of the children using the brushes creatively!

BUBBLE WRAP PRINTS

You Need: Sheets of the bubble packing wrap

Tray of paint

Paper

Printmaking

Tactile and Sensory Awareness

Creativity

Small Motor

Directions:

Tape the bubble wrap to your art table. Have paper to make prints available. Let the kids paint on the bubble wrap and then make a print of their designs!

Variation:

Do the same thing with your LEGO TABLE. Allow the children to paint on the small lego circles and then take a print of their designs.

CORNSTARCH SQUIRTING

Small Motor

Hand Strength as Precursor for Pre-Writing

Cause/Effect
(Water Changed the Powder to a Liquid)

Absorption

Wet/Dry

Hard/ Soft

Color Mixing

Creating a Suspension
(Substance that Has Property of Solid and Liquid at Same Time)

You Need: Trays

Cornstarch (I get the 25 lb. bag from a restaurant supply store)

Squirt bottles filled with colored water

Directions:

Dump cornstarch onto the trays. Allow the children to squirt the colored water onto the piles of cornstarch.

Variation:

Put the cornstarch into tubs instead of trays. Then, as the water and cornstarch begin to mix together (and turn into ooblick) it's already in a sensory tub!

SPARKLE DESIGNS

You Need: 3 cups Flour,

3 cups Salt

3 cups Water

(if you want to make a bigger batch, just remember to use equal parts)

3 colors of food coloring or liquid watercolors

3 old dish soap containers (more if you have a lot of kids!)

3 mixing bowls

Wooden spoon and maybe a funnel

Explorations of Wet/Dry

Creativity

Evaporation

Small Motor

Directions:

In each bowl mix together 1 c. water, 1 c. salt, 1 c. flour and a squirt of your favorite color. Pour each mixture into a dish soap container. You may need to use the funnel. Take your time. Best to do it before you are ready to do the activity! Allow the kids to squirt the contents of the containers onto thick sheets of paper, or onto cardboard. When they dry they look sparkley!!

UNDER THE TABLE COLORING

Stages of Scribbling

Creativity

Small Motor

Socialization

Spatial Awareness

Observations and Different Perspectives

You Need: Baskets of crayons

Paper and tape

Pillows and/or nap mats

Kid sized table(s)

Directions:

Before the children arrive, tape paper up underneath the bottom side of a table in your room. Lay some mats or a few pillows under the table. Place some crayons down there too. Resist the urge to say "HEY! Come down here. . ." Someone will find it and get down under there and figure it out!

BIKE PAINTING

You Need: Bikes, trikes and push toys
Long sheets of butcher or mural paper
A bucket of warm soapy water and sponges
A few old dish detergent bottles filled with easel paint

Large Motor Development

Creativity

Socialization

Directions:

Squirt some paint onto the paper – let the kids ride bikes through the paint making the bike tracks on the long sheet of paper! This is definitely process oriented! The bikes usually end up tearing the paper and then we turn the project into a bike wash! The kids love to wash the bikes after using them to paint their mural!

ROLLER BRUSH FLASHLIGHT PAINTING

Light/Dark Explorations

Creativity

Tracking

You Need: (To make 4)

4 cheap flashlights

4 roller brushes

Duct tape or clear packing tape

Paper and paint

Directions:

Use duct tape to attach the roller brush to the flashlight. Turn the flashlight on, dip the roller into paint and zoom zoom the roller across the paper! I've had 4 year old's tell me, "Ms. Lisa, LOOK! I'm chasing that light!"

Clean up:

Just remove the roller sponge from the roller brush. Wash it, dry it and stick it back on.

SPLATTER PAINTING

You Need: Outside easel (or drag the inside one OUT!)

Drippy but not fully diluted easel paint

Brushes

Paper

Lots and lots of space!

Large Motor (Big Arm Swoops)

Hand Eye Coordination

Creativity

Judging and Estimating
(How Far Back Should I Stand?
Where will the Paint Land?)

Directions:

In an area of the yard that has a lot of room, set up the easel. Allow the kids to move as far from the easel as they want and then fling their painty brush at their paper at the easel to make splatter prints!

Suggestion:

One year the kids called this "danger zone painting," calling the space between the painter and the easel the "danger zone." Have a change of clothes handy!

CRAYON MELTING

Cause/Effect
(Heat = Melting Crayon)

Creativity

Properties of Matter
(Solid Crayon Turns into
Melted Wax)

Observations

Small motor

You Need: Warming tray or electric griddle

Crayons with the papers removed

Paper, foil or wax paper

An old oven mitt or hot pad

Directions:

Plug in the warming tray and let it heat up. As the kids melt the crayons on their paper, foil or wax paper, they can rest their other hand **on** or **in** the oven mitt so they don't get "burned."

Need to Know:

Kids can do this everyday all day! This activity is so popular, I acquired four warming trays so that four children could be doing it at the same time. The children are allowed to make as many as they want, often making 5 or 10 in a row. They can melt until they are done. Some will design, make scribbles, write shapes, some will drop a crayon on the heat and watch it melt. Don't tell them, "That's not what it's for." Remember being process oriented is our goal.

FEET PAINTING

You Need: Feet!
Sheets of paper
Tray of paint
"Wash foot bucket"

Directions:

Allow the children to step in the paint then walk on their paper creating feet prints! Beware of slippery feet.

Clean Up:

After they are done painting I have them sit in on a chair with their feet in the wash-foot bucket. I help wash their feet and then dry them with a soft towel.

Sensory Awareness

Movement

Creativity

Balance

Self Awareness
(That's My Foot)

DIP AND DYE ART

Absorption

Creativity

Color Mixing

Exploration of Primary and Secondary Colors

You Need: Coffee filters (I get the h-u-g-e ones at Smart and Final)
Bowls filled with liquid watercolors

Directions:

Fold up, or squish up, the coffee filters. Dip them into the colors. Dip each part of the filter into a different color. Carefully open them up to see the vibrant colors!

Suggestion:

Resist the urge to make these into flowers or snowflakes! Enjoy the process in and of itself and watch the neat color mixing.

FLOWER PAINTING

You Need: Carnations (Ask a florist if they'll donate old ones ready to be
thrown-out)
Trays of paint
Paper

Creativity
Making Prints and Patterns
Sensory Awareness
(Smell of Flowers)

Directions:

Allow the children to paint with the carnations! Experiment with easel paint and
with liquid watercolor paint.

Suggestion:

Ask parents to bring in a flower on a designated day. Use some to paint with and
put some in a vase as a table centerpiece. Document the process by taking
pictures to share with the families.

DRIP DROP PRINTS

You Need: Wax paper

Paper towels

Liquid watercolor paints

Eyedroppers or pipettes

Directions:

Provide everyone with a sheet of wax paper, or simply cover the table with it. Drip-drop the paint onto the wax paper using the pipettes. The colored water will bead up on the wax paper. Place a paper towel on top of the colored beads, lift up to see the drip-drop prints.

Absorption

Color Mixing

Patterns

Inquiry and Questioning
(Why Does the Wax Paper do
That?)

Creativity

Small Motor
(Pincer Grasp Development
When Using Pipettes)

Q-TIP PAINTING

You Need: Q-tips
                  Paper
                  Trays of paint

Small Motor

Creativity

Design

Patterns

Directions:

Allow the children to paint with the Q-tips.

Remember:

Some kids will make dots, some will make long lines, and some kids will jump up, get the glue and make q-tip collages! That's OK too. I tease the kids by saying that the only thing they should put in their ear is their elbow! There are always a lot of giggles as they try to do this!

GLITTER AND GLUE

Small Motor

Pattern/Placement

Creativity

Line/Design

You Need: Glitter

Glue

Paper

Directions:

Allow the children to make glue designs and then sprinkle glitter onto the glue.

Hints:

If the glitter shaker has TONS of holes, cover a few up with masking tape. Make a "dump plate" where the kids can dump off the extra glitter. You can then put this glitter back into the glitter shaker. Don't worry about keeping the glitter colors all separate, mixing the glitter is OK! Color your glue by adding some liquid watercolor to the glue and shaking it until it's mixed.

Remember:

Glitter and glue is one of those projects that the kids can do every day all day!

TILE BLOCK PRINTS

You Need: 12 x 12 x 1/2 inch square piece of wood (makes one tile block)

Scrap tiles or you can purchase them from Home Depot

Liquid nails (also purchased at Home Depot)

Paint and paper

Printing

Cause/Effect
(Painting + Lifting Off = Printing)

Shape Exploration

Creativity

Directions:

Use the Liquid Nails to adhere the tiles to the wood. After drying and setting for 24 hours allow the children to paint on the tiles, then place a paper on top and make a print. The more varied the chunks of tile, the more varied the designs!

Hints:

I always have at least 4 tile blocks available so that 4 kids can be using them. Also, don't worry about cleaning them spotless between uses! Kids don't mind the colors!

Variations:

If you have a Lego table available, allow the children to paint on the Lego "dots" and then lift prints off of the designs they paint there too.

RECORD PLAYER SPIN ART

Tracking (Watch it Spin)

Creativity

Small Motor

You Need: A record player

Paper plates – punch or cut a hole in the middle

Crayons, markers or watercolor paints

Directions:

Put the paper plate on the turn table. As the turntable spins let the kids paint, crayon or draw on the spinning plate!

Suggestions:

Play with the speed of the record player and see what happens! Look for old turntables at garage sales or at the Salvation Army.

NOSE PAINTING

You Need: The mirror from the dress up center or some hand held ones

Paint

Small brushes

Socialization

Creativity

Self Awareness

(My Nose)

Directions:

Let the kids paint their noses and then make prints on the paper! This activity causes gales of laughter! Often times the kids want to paint each other's noses! I have them ask each other, "Can I paint your nose?" or "Will you paint my nose?"

Clean up:

I have a box of baby-wipes for quick clean up.

Suggestion:

Worried about the painty noses that might go home? Have a Polaroid camera on hand so parents can see the excitement and creativity that happened that day!

LIPSTICK KISSES

You Need: A bunch of sticks of old lipsticks,
or ones you find on sale, or ones a few of the
moms might donate. Know an Avon lady?

Paper

Mirrors

Sorry Guys!
This One's Just Plain Fun!

Directions:

Let the kids put lipstick on their lips and then smooch the paper! Again, like nose painting, this produces the giggles! Have that Polaroid ready to capture the smiles! Have baby wipes ready for easy clean up. And have that dress up center mirror near by, kids love to see their lips after they put on the lipstick!

HAT PAINTING

You Need: An old construction hat or an old T-ball or little league helmet

Duck tape

Paintbrush

Directions:

Duck tape the paintbrush to the rim of the helmet! As the children wear the hat allow them to dip it into a tray of paint and use the hat brush to paint at the easel. It looks easy but it can be kind of tricky! Most of the kids will hold the hat on with their hands while moving their bodies all around to make their painting.

Got two hats? Hook them together with a wire coat hanger and duct tape. Watch as two children paint together. Now THAT takes problem solving and negotiation skills!

Visual Skills

Problem Solving
(Hat on Head - How to
get Paint?)

Creativity

Large Motor
(Try It—You'll See How Much
the Whole Body is involved)

MAGNET PAINTING

You Need: Magnet wands

Magnet balls

Paper clips

Paper plates

Liquid watercolor paint

Eyedroppers or pipettes

Magnet Exploration
(Negative and Positive)

Questioning and Inquiry
(Why Does it "Stick" to Some
Things but Not to Others?)

Creativity

Hand-Eye Coordination

Directions:

Drip drop some watercolor onto the paper plate and put a few magnet balls or paper clips into the watercolor. With one hand hold the paper plate and with the other hold the magnet wand UNDER the paper plate. Drag the paper clip and magnet balls around and around through the paint. It might take a minute for smaller hands to get the hand of it, but they do!

FLUBBER GAK

You Need: 5 TBS Borax
2 cups Elmers glue
1 ½ cups water to mix with the glue
an additional 1 cup of (hot) water to mix with the Borax
Liquid watercolor or food coloring (if color is desired)

Directions:

Mix 2 cups of glue and 1 ½ cup water in a big bowl. Add color if desired
and stir. In the extra cup of hot water, dissolve the 5 TBS of Borax. Stir it
well. After it's dissolved, pour the Borax mixture slowly (and a little at a time) into
the glue and water mixture. Watch it coagulate! Mix with your hands or a sturdy
wooden spoon. At first it is wet and slimy, but keep kneading until it becomes one
big flubber gak ball! It will keep in an airtight container or ziploc for a few weeks.
When it begins to flick apart or get too hard, it is time to make a new batch

Suggestion:

I prepare this at home and bring it into class already made. This decreases the
chance of anyone "accidentally" getting into the Borax.

Try This:

Use straws to blow big flubber bubbles!

P.S. Soak fabric in vinegar to remove GAK from clothes

Exploration of Air
(Blowing Bubble)

Changing of Properties

Cause/Effect
(Liquid + Borax = Gak)

Squeezing = Small Motor
Development and Hand Strength

COTTON PUFF ART

You Need: Cotton balls

                  Paint

                  Paper

                  Glue (optional)

Tactile and Sensory Exploration

Small Motor
(Pulling the Cotton Apart)

Creativity

Directions:

Let the kids paint with the cotton balls on big sheets of paper. Allow them to glue some to the paper for added texture if they want.

Suggestions:

Attach a clothespin to a few of the cotton balls for the kids who do not want to get their fingers painty. Resist the urge to cut the paper into cloud shapes! Let the inspiration come from the kids!

I used to cut out tons of baby blue "clouds." Once, after I had changed my mind about how to approach children's art, a child in my class got up, got himself a pair of scissors and cut out his own "cloud." He asked for black and white paint and made a gray cloud. He told me, "It's an angry cloud – it's stormy." It had rained the night before. That wouldn't have happened if I had already decided that the clouds were blue, pretty and puffy!!!

EASEL PAINTING:

A few words about easel painting:

1. your easel should be available each and every day
2. there should be an easel of some sort outside
3. clothes-pinning paper to a chain link fence is an easel
4. if you are short on space you can mount easels to an inside wall
5. taping paper to a garage wall, the playroom wall, or even the back fence, is an easel

To vary the experiences at the easel:

1. add scents to the easel paint
2. cut holes in the easel paper for negative space experiments
3. have a bandanna or a scarf close-by for blindfold painting
4. add cornmeal, sand or sawdust to the easel paints

Socialization

Stages of Scribbling

Small Motor

Creativity

Self Expression

SLIDE PAINTING

You Need: A playground slide

Roll of butcher paper

Plastic balls, tennis balls, dog toy balls, etc.

Tray of paint

Directions:

Tape the paper to the slide. Put the tray of paint and the balls at the top of the slide. Allow the children to roll the painty balls down the slide into the sand and dirt below! Don't have a big slide? Use the small ones that are attached to toddler and preschool plastic climbers. Don't have any slides? Get some boxes and a long sheet of plywood and make an inclined plane!

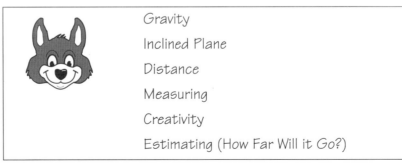

Gravity

Inclined Plane

Distance

Measuring

Creativity

Estimating (How Far Will it Go?)

SUN PRINTS

You Need: A sunny day

Colored construction paper

Blocks

Directions:

Bring the kids, blocks and paper all outside before nap on a warm sunny day. Allow the children to put their paper down on the sidewalk, the driveway or playground and then place a few blocks wherever they want on their paper. After they wake up have them check out their papers and see what happened while they were napping! The sun will fade the paper surrounding the blocks, but will leave prints of where the blocks were placed.

Cause/Effect
(Paper + Sun + Blocks =
Prints on Paper)

Creativity

Questioning and Inquiring
(Why?)

EGG CARTON COLORING

You Need: Lots of styrofoam egg cartons

Liquid watercolors or food coloring in beakers or other cups

Pipettes

Directions:

Set the egg cartons out on the table. Fill each with a small amount of water. This allows the kids to watch the water turn colors. Set the beakers out with pipettes and simply allow the children to experiment with color mixing. Allow the children to dump out the colored water and "get fresh" whenever they want.

Suggestions:

I keep a small child-sized pitcher of water so the kids can refill their own egg carton!

Small Motor Skills
Pipettes = Pincer Grasp Strength
Color Mixing
Primary and Secondary Color Exploration

LIQUID LAYERS

You Need: Small clear party punch cups

Pink shampoo (I use the Suave Strawberry kind)

Blue dishwashing soap (Dawn)

Any color of colored water (I usually make green)

Cooking oil (yellow)

Density (Weight of Each Liquid)

Questioning and Inquiring
(How Does that Happen?
Why do They Layer up the Same
way Each time?)

Observation Skills

Directions:

Pour the 5 ingredients into the cups in any order. Watch how they all separate out in the same pattern no matter which one you pour in first or second! I would let the kids each "make" one, then we would put them on a shelf with a lot of sun or on a window ledge. They look great when the light catches them.

Suggestion:

If someone wants to take one home, cover with saran wrap and a rubberband.

SNAIL TRAILS

Animal Science

Gentle Hands

Color Mixing

Creativity

You Need: Snails from the garden

Paper

Tray of liquid watercolor paints (you can use food coloring too)

Directions:

Dip the snails into the colored water and allow them to make snail trails across the paper! The paint is non-toxic, as is the food coloring. This project does not harm the snails.

Suggestion:

I will put out magnifying glasses and clear safety goggles too. These extra props can really enhance the experience. When done, release the snails into the yard, grass or playground.

FEET DANCING

You'll Need: Feet!

Fabric paint

The kid's favorite music

A sheet (to be used as your picnic sheet)

Directions:

Let the kids carefully step into a tray of fabric paint and then dance to their favorite music! One year the favorite was Greg and Steve's "Listen and Move" and the next year the kids loved to dance the Macarena! After they are done feet dancing on the sheet you can wash the sheet and then use it for picnics or group time or whatever! The fabric paint will not wash off.

Dancing to the music!

Large Motor

Socialization

Creativity

Self Awareness (My Feet! Our Sheet!)

TOILET PAPER TOSS

You Need: Many many rolls of TP

Lots of room

Plenty of time

Large Motor (Big Arm Movements and Lots of Running)

More/Less

Socialization

Cause/Effect
(Throw Paper = Paper Unrolls)

Directions:

Provide each child with full roll of TP as you enter the place where you will have your TP toss. I often use the yard, playground, living room, classroom, or cafeteria. Let them toss it, throw it, wrap each other up in it, wrap themselves up in it!

It is a high-energy yet cooperative activity. Sometimes I put some music on, sometimes not. As we are cleaning up we save the TP rolls to blow bubbles with and we save the TP for making clean mud! (see page 74)

GLITTER PLATES

You Need: Paper plates
Elmers glue
Sequins and sparkles
Flashlights

Light/Dark Exploration
Reflection of Colors
Socialization

Directions:

Allow the children to glue the sequins all over their plate. After they all dry, take all the kids and a bunch of flashlights into a dark room. Whether the bathroom, kitchen, closet, cozy spot under the stairs, WHEREVER it is dark enough to have all the kids shine the light onto their plates and then reflect the colored sparkles onto the wall! A white wall works best.

Beautiful kaleidoscope effects!

PENDULUM PAINTING

Creativity

Hand/Eye Coordination

Tracking

Small Motor

You Need: Paintbrushes and trays of paint

Paper taped to the floor

Masking tape, scissors and some long string

Directions:

Cut long pieces of string and then tape them to the handle part of the brushes. You want the brush to be suspended from the string. Allow the children to dip the hanging brush into the paint and then swing their brushes back and forth over their paper to paint in a pendulum style motion.

Helpful Hint:

Some of the children will swing their brushes at first and then squat down and paint. Some will just sit down and paint from the beginning. Remember this process is OK too!

HOSE PHONE
A.K.A. THREE WAY CALLING

You Need: A long old hose
Duct tape
A PVC pipe "T" connector
Three funnels
Scissors

Socialization
Sound Exploration
Vibrations
Volume and Pitch of Voice

Directions:

Cut the hose into three equal sections. Use the duct tape to connect each section to the PVC "T" connector. Now duct tape the funnels to the other end of each hose section to use as the phone part. Ta-da! Three way calling!

Suggestion:

If you do not have extra funnels you can cut a soda bottle in half and use the use the top piece as a recycled funnel!

THE EXTRA LAP

You Need: An old big pair of jeans
Batting (fabric stuffing)
Velcro or sewing machine

This is Another "Simply Fun" One!

Enjoy!

Directions:

Velcro closed or sew up the bottoms of the pant legs. Stuff each leg and the butt part with fabric batting. Then Velcro the waist together! Now you have an extra lap for your cozy corner and book center. (The top is velcro'd so you can wash the jeans if necessary)

ZIPLOC SQUISH BAGS

You Need: Ziploc style baggies

Many assorted squishy items
like hair gel, shaving cream, cool whip,
applesauce, cotton balls, corn syrup, etc etc –
the list is endless!!

Small Motor

Tactile and Sensory Exploration

Squishing Facilitates Hand
Strength (Prewriting)

Color Mixing

Directions:

Fill the bags with the squishy items before the kids get to class – allow them to squish and feel them.

Make sure you have enough bags! Some may break with active exploration!

SHAVING CREAM AND WATER

Density

Color Mixing

Observation

Small Motor Development
Using the Pipettes

You Need: A clear large container

(I use the clear acrylic food storage containers from Smart and Final)

Shaving cream

Beakers & pipettes

Liquid watercolors or food coloring

Directions:

Fill your container 3/4 full with water. Make colored water in your beakers. Squirt shaving cream on top of the water. Allow the children to drip-drop colors onto the shaving cream. Watch how the colors sink through the shaving cream and change the color of the water below!

Suggestions:

Some kids will begin "stirring" the shaving cream with the pipettes and watch the colors swirl around, this is OK! Some will want to dump it out and "make fresh," this is OK too.

OOBLICK

You Need: Cornstarch

Water

Sensory tub

Directions:

This ooey gooey sensory recipe is an equal mixture of cornstarch and water. In your sensory tub, dump about 10 cups of cornstarch. Have 10 cups of water in a pitcher. Slowly pour the water in and allow the kids to mix with their hands. Don't just dump the water in because sometimes you DO NOT need to use all the water! Better to need more then make cornstarch soup!! You can leave it in your tub all week. Do NOT cover it – it will get moldy. As it dries out during the week, simply reconstitute with more water. One of my all time favorites!

Properties of Substance

Cause/Effect (Cornstarch + Water = Goop)

Solids and Liquids

Ooblick is a Suspension as it has the properties of a Solid and Liquid at the Same Time

Small Motor (Squeezing of the Ooblick Increases Hand Strength)

KNOX GELATIN MOLD

You Need: A plastic container, any size, to serve as your mold

A ratio of 3/4 cups of water to 1 packet of Knox gelatin

Saucepan & wooden spoon

Pam, or any other kind, non-stick spray

Pipettes and liquid watercolor

Directions:

Fill your chosen container with water. Then measure out how many CUPS of water the container held. Pour the water into the saucepan and dry out the mold with a paper towel. Then spray your mold with the non-stick spray. DIVIDE the number of cups of water by .75. This will tell you how many packets of knox that you need for this sized container. Over low heat, stir the packets into the water. After it dissolves, carefully pour it into your container. Let set for a few hours or over night. Allow the children to inject the knox mold with pipettes and eyedroppers filled with colored water!

 Small Motor Development

Pipettes Facilitate Pincer Grasp

Creativity

Chemistry—Reactions While "Cooking" the Knox

Properties of Liquids (Liquid to Solid)

PLAYDOUGH

You Need: 3 cups flour

1½ cups salt

3 cups water (colored if desired)

5 TBS oil

6 tsp Cream of tartar

I double this recipe when making it for class

Small Motor Development

Dramatic Play

Socialization

Creativity

Directions:

Mix all of the ingredients together in a bowl. I use my electric hand mixer. Pour the dough mixture into the pan on the stove. Stirring constantly, cook over med-low heat until a ball forms. Take out of the pan and knead. When cool, store in airtight container or ziploc.

Variations:

1. Add used coffee grounds to the mixture **before** you cook.
2. Add glitter to it **after** it's been cooked.

Remember:

Allow the children to explore playdough with "just" their hands too; they do not always need playdough toys and tools.

COFFEE SAND

You Need: 4 cups dried, used, coffee grounds

2 cups cornmeal

1 cup flour

1/2 cup salt

Sensorial Awareness

Tactile Awareness

Textures

Scooping, Pouring and Dumping all Facilitate the Development of Piaget's Concept of Conservation

Directions:

Dry out the used coffee grounds by placing the grounds in a big pan or on a cookie sheet, and putting them in your oven on LOW heat for about an hour. Then mix all ingredients together in your sensory tub for scooping, pouring, feeling and smelling! Store coffee sand in a big covered container so that you can use it again and again.

Suggestion:

Ask your local gourmet coffee shop to save their grounds for a day for you. Provide them with a container and be sure to pick it up when you say you'll be back! I always have a freezer bag full of the dried used grounds . . . . just in case!!

RAINBOW STEW

You Need: 4-6 cups of cornstarch

1 cup sugar

12 cups water

Saucepan & wooden spoon

Plastic containers & Ziploc bags

Liquid watercolors or food coloring (I like to use the primary colors for this one).

Color Mixing

Small Motor

Observation Skills

Cooking is Chemistry

Directions:

In a saucepan, mix the water and sugar. Slowly add the cornstarch one cup at a time. Make sure to keep stirring! The reaction of the ingredients takes time. When the mixture begins looking like creamy, white mashed potatoes, turn off the heat and divide the "stew" into separate bowls. Add color while it's still warm and then allow it to cool if you are using it right away. If you are making it for the next day, put it in the fridge overnight. To use it, scoop spoonfuls of the colored "stew" into Ziploc bags and let the kids squish!

COLORED SPAGHETTI

Sensory and Tactile
Explorations

Cutting Skills

Small Motor

You Need: 1 lb. Pasta (I get the cheap stuff)

2 cups cooking oil

Liquid watercolors

Containers

Directions:

In a big saucepan, cook the pasta with the 2 cups of oil. Cook it as though you were going to eat it. When done, strain it, divide it into bowls and color it with food coloring or liquid watercolors. No need to add alcohol to color the pasta.

When the pasta has cooked off put it in the sensory tub for lots of squishy exploration.

Suggestion:

The children love cutting it with scissors, squishing it and even painting with it! If it's out all day long – toss it at the end of the day. If it's only out for a little while, you can freeze it for another time. Dispose of it when it gets stinky!

OUTSIDE SOUNDS

You Need: Pots & pans
Washboards
Hubcaps
Metal tubs
Metal trash can lids, etc.

One of the many engaging activities at the Roseville Community Preschool

Directions:

Hang these objects from low trees, or secure them in another fashion so as to allow exploration of sounds and vibrations. Allow the children to tap and bang on them in order to hear the different tones. Each object sounds different, even the six different hubcaps we have hanging have six distinctive sounds!

Suggestion:

Always be on the lookout for any kind of object that may make a good sound when thumped! We have found numerous treasures on the side of the freeway!

Auditory Development

Music, Sounds and Vibration

Socialization

Patterns and Rhythm

A glimpse of our play yard

119

SPAGHETTI PAINTING/TOSS

You Need: Cooked spaghetti (either colored or plain)
Sensory tub
Mural paper
2 or 3 colors of easel paint
A lot of space!

Directions:

Tape or adhere the mural paper on an outside wall or fence. Put the cooked spaghetti in the sensory tub, squirt a few globs of paint in the tub along with the spaghetti. Allow the kids to toss the spaghetti at their "target" of the mural paper!

Helpful Hints:

This is a good outside project. Clean up is simple too. Wait until the sun has dried out the noodles, then rake or scoop them up.

Large Motor (Big Arm Movements)

Tracking

Hand-Eye Coordination

Creativity

Judging Distance and Estimating (How Far Back do I Need to Be?)

BAKING SODA AND VINEGAR EXPLORATIONS

You Need: Baking soda & vinegar

KOOLAID (optional)

Pie tins (have enough for your group!)

Pipettes & beakers

Liquid watercolors or food coloring (optional)

Dish soap (optional)

Visual Observations

Cause/Effect
Vinegar + Baking Soda =
Carbon Dioxide

All the Senses are Engaged!
Touch, Smell, Taste, Listen
and See

Directions:

Put baking soda in the pie tins and vinegar in the beakers. Allow the children to drip-drop vinegar onto the baking soda. SEE the bubbles! SMELL the vinegar! LISTEN to the fizzing! All of the senses are engaged while you are making carbon dioxide!

Variations:

1. Mix some Kool-aid into the baking soda.

2. Add liquid watercolor or food coloring to the vinegar.

3. Add a teaspoon of dish soap to the vinegar.

CONTACT PAPER AND
BUBBLE WRAP ON THE FLOOR

Sensory and Tactile Exploration

Large Motor Skill Development

You Need: Contact Paper

Masking tape

Bubble Wrap

A big space

Directions:

Tape the **BUBBLE WRAP** onto an area of your floor where the kids have room to move and pop the bubbles either with their hands or their feet.

In another area, carefully open up a big sheet of **CONTACT PAPER** and tape it onto your floor STICKY SIDE UP! The children really like to walk all over the contact paper with their bare feet. It makes a squish squish sound! Some kids want to touch with their hands – not feet – that's OK too.

SHAKER BOTTLES

You Need: Recycled water bottles

Liquid watercolors or food coloring

Cooking oil

Glitter

Dish soap

A few extra marbles

Hot glue gun (or access to one)

Depending on What You Put in the Bottles You Can Attach Many Concepts:
1) Oil & Water=Density
2) Marbles & Water=Audio Discrimination

3) Soap & Water=Cause/Effect & Visual Observations

Directions:

Fill up the recycled bottles with water. Color the water anyway you want. Make a few bottles a mix of glitter and water, a few oil and water bottles, a couple of colored water and dish soap (shake this one hard!) and a few with colored water and marbles! Hot glue the lids back on to the bottle and viola! Colorful sensorial shaker bottles!

FISH PRINTS

You Need: A scaly fish (or two) from the butcher

Paint

Paper

Printing

Color Mixing

Pattern

Design

Creativity

Directions:

Allow the children to paint on the fish! Then place a paper on top of the fish to lift up a fish print!

Reminders:

Can be kind of stinky! Throw the fish away when you are finished! Also, even if you do not like the project, or don't want to touch the fish, I guarantee that SOMEONE in the class won't mind doing it for you!

Hints:

Fish with lots of scales make the best prints. Look for fish of different sizes and shapes for the most variation.

ICE AND ROCK SALT

You Need: Blocks of ice
You can either purchase them or freeze water in every imaginable
container the night before

Rock Salt
Containers of colored water
Pipettes or eyedroppers

Cause/Effect
(Salt Melts the Water)

Small Motor Pincer
Development Using Pipettes

Properties of Water
(Liquid-Solid-Liquid)

Creativity

Freezing/Melting

Color Mixing

Questioning and Inquiring
(Why! Why! Why!)

Directions:

Place the blocks of ice in a sensory tub. Sprinkle the rock salt on top of the ice.
The rock salt will makes holes in the ice! Allow the children to drip drop
colored water onto the ice and into the holes!

Variations:

You can use bags of ice, smaller cubes of ice and table salt too!

SENSORY TUB IDEAS

Tactile and Sensory Exploration

Scooping, Pouring and Measuring

Conservation

Small Motor

Socialization

Fill your sensory tubs with any of the ingredients and materials listed below. Right now with the toddlers I like to have the same thing out all week and then rotate to something new. I also always have two tubs available for exploration; one filled with something wet and ooey and the other filled with something dry. Honor (as often as possible) the requests from older kids who have favorite sensory tub activities! Be sure to put out long wooden spoons for the children who don't want to touch (with their hands) your sensory substances!

Try any of these things and remember to always be thinking of other things you can add too!

Mud	Water	Raw pumpkin
Dirt	Cornstarch	Coffee sand *(pg. 116)*
Sand	Flax seed with water	Bubbles *(pg. 69)*
Sand and shells	Shaving cream	Corks
Bird seed	Paper to cut	Pudding
Cooked spaghetti	Clean Mud *(pg. 74)*	Rice & Beans
Ooblick *(pg. 113)*	Cornmeal	Flour

Bird Seed & Cornmeal

Water, Tubes & Funnels

Flour & Beans

Flour & Rice

Water & Gutter

Water, Pots & Pans

127

INDEX OF ACTIVITY IDEAS

For assistance in locating and/or purchasing any of the materials, paint, paper, craft supplies, etc, referenced in the activity section, please contact

The Learning Through Adventure Company

Phone: (800) 477-7977

Email: LTAC@ooeygooey.com

Web: www.ooeygooey.com

REFERENCES

DIMIDJIAN, *Victoria. Play's Place in Public Education for Young Children.* Washington, D.C.: National Education Association, 1992.

HEALY, Jane. *Endangered Minds, Why Children Don't Think and What We Can Do About It.* New York: Touchstone Simon and Schuster, 1990.

MATE, Ferenc. *A Reasonable Life. Toward a Simpler, Secure, More Humane Existence.* New York: Albatross Publishing, 1993.

PEARCE, Joseph Chilton. *Evolution's End. Claiming the Potential of Our Intelligence.* New York: Harper Collins, 1992.

RIVKIN, Mary S. *The Great Outdoors. Restoring Children's Right to Play Outside.* Washington, D.C.: National Association for the Education of Young Children, 1995.

The Ooey Gooey Lady in Person

Lisa Murphy, *the ooey gooey lady,* has been an early childhood educator for over fifteen years. She has worked with children in various environments including Head Start programs, private preschools, family childcare and kindergartens. She earned her B.S. degree in Human Services and Counseling from Cal State University, Fullerton and is the owner and director of The Learning Through Adventure Company, an educational consulting firm. Lisa presents over 150 workshops each year to audiences across the country! Don't miss out! Call Lisa to schedule a workshop in your area today!

Phone: (800) 477-7977

Email: LTAC@ooeygooey.com

Web: www.ooeygooey.com

Workshops Currently Available:

• What if Today Was Their Only Day? (keynote)

• Ooey Gooey Squishy Plop!   Hands-on play for every day!

• Many Kinds of Smart! Understanding Multiple Intelligences Theory

• Creative Art With Young Children! It's the process NOT the product!

• The Importance of Early Experiences.. how playing IS getting them ready for school!

• Making Time for Books and Stories

• Fizzle Bubble Pop and WOW!   Simple Science for Young Children

• What to say when the wolves come knockin'! Linking a hands-on philosophy to educational standards